MOON POEMS AND OTHER DEATHLESS SONGS

by

Andrew Lafleche

Books by

ANDREW LAFLECHE

Ashes

No Diplomacy

Shameless

A Pardonable Offence

One Hundred Little Victories

On Writing

Merica, Merica on the Wall

After I Turn into Alcohol

Eyes Wide

Ride

Grateful acknowledgment is made to the following publications where some of these poems first appeared: Bywords, In Parentheses, Barren Magazine, Ekstasis Editions, White Wall Review, PCC Inscape Literary Magazine, *and* The Internet Void.

Contents

Blow Smoke at the Moon

they come for the light
moon brighter under red wine
longing to be owned

sunshine abandoned
the pulse in static resounds
weather the skins new

a moon-ray's heartbeat
alone on a mountain bluff
can it be conquered?

the night I concluded:
if I could kill Christ, I would,
you called. again.

The Silence

there is the silence to be thankful for
there are shooting stars and pulsing satellites
the dogs don't bark into the night, that's always a plus

still, they stare at me with pleading eyes
most days the lights from the city cloud space
and if someone lurks outside, the dogs'll bark fiercely

I'll take the silence any day
the hum of the refrigerator
or the buzz of the bathroom fan after a shit

the dogs licking their dog beds
the printer chewing away at lines
the keyboard clacking with each word

it's not really silence, but it's something

The Ring Around the Moon

a perfect circle
shadows cast lay atop
shadows already at rest.

stars seen in depth
sadden me, staring into a time
long passed; how to move forward
always looking back?

it hasn't always been this way
or maybe like stars
appearing eternal, burn bright
until one day they don't,
I will, too.

this moment admiring the moon,
contemplating after
all those bottles of wine,
battling melancholy and sadness
as my shotgun lies on the table
shells strewn across the room.

and then I wake
overtaken by stark blackness
open eyes, no light coming through.

chaos, my mind, end of its tether
voices, familiar ones
afar, muffled by the ringing in my ears.

consoling voices, assuring
voices, voices that parrot
"everything is going to be okay,"
but if everything was,
I wouldn't feel afraid like I do.

the ringing isn't a dinner bell
or alarm clock, but the droning hum
a gunshot echo inside four walls.

lying in darkness I question:
have I shot someone? have there been people here?
have I shot myself? is this what dying feels like?
why can't I see? why the ringing in my ears?

I can smell: burnt eggs.

I can feel: a hand pressed against my face
another supports my shoulder.

I recognize the sobbing voice
but hear it as a stranger's
and even if I could make it out
I don't want to.

questions continue:
could it be paramedics? a police officer?
am I in trouble? I am in trouble.
decide to stop trying.

this is trouble and if I am to live,
best to delay consequences
for as long as possible.

what is more embarrassing
than surviving a suicide?
or a homicide suicide?

I thought of the mess to be cleaned
by someone who'd rather not:
blood spray on the walls, on the mirror
pieces of gray matter stuck to the patio doors
overlooking the river.
the resale value will plummet.

why can't I remember?
who are these voices? why can't I see?
aware of thinking and recognition of
thinking thoughts.
existing on two planes I fight
to make sense of the question
above all questions: why?

letting go.
if this is suicide, years of torment
are moments away from nothingness.
if criminal offense, there is no escape.

I drift off, let go, mumble something
the ringing stops
my pain disappears with the voices

for the first time I exist in silence,
without torment, without noise,
floating on my back in the ocean
ears submerged.

if this be death,
welcome.

At Least They're Not Terrors, Anymore

Woke with a gash across my hand, other
tiny scratches—fogged, even though I'd been
asleep nine hours, give or take 30 or
60 minutes—and minus those two times
I sat up; one for the incredible
clarity of a luminous moon, once
to silence the eight-a.m. alarm on
my Timex resting on the window ledge.

Did I dream of war? Shoulders and chest and
kidneys and lumbar, pained to touch and strained
to move, despite lack of heart racing—the
physical symptoms of combat, acute.
A battle with ghosts, like over there. I
laugh, swing my feet to meet the cool wood floor,
like over there, I know not what happened.
At least they are not terrors anymore.

Patricia

It may have been the moon, first phase of its
Newness in the blue twilight sky—maybe;
Could have been the cool breeze, the relentless
Assault of mosquitos—it wasn't now,
Then, when I was there, Mexico, lying
On the chilled sand, with her: Patricia.

That first night together in the darkness
The morning aft, embraced in a cocoon
Hammock, chest and arms and legs sun-kissed bronze,
My clothed midline, same as when I arrived
Four weeks prior—pulled back, stole another
Look, "Is that your real color?" and giggled

As if she'd witnessed the funniest thing.
"You are so-oh white! Never seen so white!"
I smile remembering our romance—
Days shared at the beach, swimming in the nude,
She insisted I *needed* more sunshine—
Sucking on fresh mangos, paddling the

Mangroves. The glimpse of a passing moment.

Savior

Where are you going but that side of morn'?
Have I something to take its place—Follow.
Never trust a stranger who says *trust me*…
Only,
    trust me
        you must
            this time
                that side.
Take my hand, here, I'll light the flame, look-see.
Now doesn't that feel better, don't you feel—

The Fighting

Jarred from sleep, the dispatching snap
Of a bullet I didn't see coming—

Only there are no bullets here—
Only the panicked cry of an expiring mouse
Trapped beneath the floor, defeated—

Entreating sleep resume; a grateful smile;
The battlefield is miles away, now,
Across land and seas.

For not in dreams, each night, something
Must die for life to remain living, in me.

Ashes

I know I will survive this, it's what I do
doesn't mean it's without hurt
doesn't mean with each foolish knockdown
I don't question how many blows a man can take
living this life of accumulating losses:

    mittens my kitten under the passing car, Erica (my first kiss)
to the boy in the grade above, Aaron my sidekick if I knew
where he went, a skateboard, a ball glove, a taser, a quarter
pound of weed, my watch after the hooker left, my wedding ring,
my wife, dreamless nights, a batch of cabernet sauvignon, nine
days in Vegas, the first time in jail, the job with the newspaper,
that deconstructed handstitched Italian blazer, everything I'd
written before two thousand and ten, a bottle of Johnny Walker
blue I know I didn't drink, the clippings reporting Thompson's
suicide, that tattered copy of the anarchist cookbook, the hearing
in one of my ears, eight years in the army, my mind

one of the saints or buddha or Christ
said life's about learning to let go
better than everything happens for a reason
sometimes prudent to leave the pieces on the ground
carelessness with glass leads to unnecessary bleeding
this fools lament disguised as wisdom
things I was once so sure of I no longer believe:

    Santa clause and his elves, that you can grow up to be
whatever you want, humans are basically good, it's important to
have goals, god answers prayers, tell the truth, invest in the

future, blowjobs from women are always better than those from men, majority rules, you can't judge a book by its cover, I love you is unconditional, suicide is a coward's way out, if you don't trust people you make them untrustworthy, toilets flush backwards in Australia, the golden rule, free will, life has meaning, it's important to discover your passion, the news on T.V. is objective, happiness can be caught, eating vegetarian doesn't feel like being hungry, this too shall pass

the sun doesn't scare the shadows away
the light casts these tethered crude images onto
a space to be trampled by another's step
each drifting into sleep begs the gods to let me be
the edge of the cliff is staring into a foggy abyss
one gust of wind would do, what is wanted eludes:

dreams that don't end in falling awake, to be able to read the Koran without falling asleep, Taylor Swift, a retraction of all apologies, the innocents abroad by mark twain, a night with Mylie, Hermann's journey to the east, a beer or twelve preferably cold, matt's ex-girlfriend from high school, a carton of cigarettes, a view of the northern lights, to wake to the sound and the smell of the ocean, a margarita, a pitcher of margaritas, fresh fruit for breakfast, her in a white button down and nothing else, to read catcher for the first time, to read anything that isn't recommended by Orpah or you, grilled cheese with ketchup, crispy sweet potato fries, a shot of tequila, a trigger to pull

all I wanted was another ten ounces of wine
I was sure there was at least one more bottle
the last glass went over the side, shattered
a straw, the camel, my broken back

Suspended, Morning Aft

Oh, painted window of stubborn glass,
Permit this rock against your pane!

How thou mock me, this wretched morn,
Death to the sun, Evermore! Again.

Uncle Danny

they robbed him at gunpoint
the story goes
me, sitting meters from the
ocean's edge studying a decaying
biped's abating shadow
I light a pall mall, tongue the
smoldering menthol, let it linger
he'd been sober three years

when I was a child, I heard
the story: he was shot by a cop
who was deputy to my grandfather
it was a botched break and entry
of the local hardware store

during my teenage years, a drug
dealer robbed him, pierced his
cheek with a corkscrew, broke
his leg above the knee, currently
he needs a cane to walk

this grebe wasn't dead here
yesterday. there's a vulture
tearing at it, the tide is approaching
sit long enough and things begin
to settle, until the winds pick up

at the harbor's entrance is a
sunken pirate ship, only its nest

visible. this morning I jumped
into a sinking fishing boat to
bail water until we reached shore
the wind is hard-wearing these days
raging above these blooded oceans

now, years later they've robbed him
again, at gunpoint, three people
in his own apartment
beat him into a viscous pool
of his own blood, broke his skull
left him to be picked at by fowl

he's in intensive care
he's lost an eye
sober three years

I pick up my beer, light another
cigarette and skirt the edge
where the tide consumes the sand
and count the dead birds until
I reach ten

Peerless Handcuff Co.

I've had those Model 300's
tightened around my wrists,
Hands behind my back, processed:
fingerprints, pictures, tats;
Locked in a concrete room
with a concrete bed, and a stainless
bowl, lidless
like the sheetless slab. Once,
This has happened to me.
And the bitch is lucky I didn't kill her for it.

Famine

tell me something
I don't already know

about quivering grass
ahead of the storm

of screaming chicks
in their nest as the marten
claws along the branches

tell me the world is beautiful
romanticize it by excluding:

polio : tsunamis : infant death

yes, tell me more
blind me with your infatuation

have me believe as you believe
all that is too good to be truth

just spare me tomorrow

Give It All to the Night

I planted your tree
beside my pillow
and dream it roots each night

sometimes there's rocks
and sometimes there's ants
and. and. sometimes it sprouts
and: those are my favorite eves…

so, I dare these dreams
again, and again,
        wishing, one dawn
your tree becomes   you.

L— 3:16

I fell from a dream, alone in darkness
Splayed sheets, clinging to your pillow, again.

Five more minutes, I begged
Just five more, please—

Woke, you, towel taught
Wrapped around your waist

My hands traced your skin
Rested on your face;
Observed the apology on your lips

Exposing the dream for the lie it was—
You whispered in my ear nary a word:

Dissolved into another night, damning
Me to relive the memory, withal.

Sometimes

Sometimes my eyes play tricks and I believe
To see the stars expanding in the night.
I stare at the Milky Way cloud for shots,
Meteors scraping the surface of sky.
Convince myself their depth, as telephone
Poles shrink over the length of a long road,
Ever moving—Time—Ever standing still.

Sometimes times I drown her at night
—Sometimes twice.
Light a cigarette, inhale, and let go;
Four bottles later, when stars are not stars,
Anymore—If they ever were—Home gone.

Sometimes the last glass is there to sleep to,
Placed on the cork coaster beside my bed
—Security like some women have kids
In defense of whatever fear writhes near—
Knowing I won't drink it, but just in case,
Comfort in the glass of Cabernet; though,
Sometimes, I wait on sleep, longing never
To wake again with the rouge rising dawn.

A Face

of one thousand lives
stares back at me
perspiration
on brow
moist beneath the eyes

a mirrored face
of a thousand more
to come

weighted like a pine
in winter
bowed with snow
reaching
toward the ground

melting in wait
of the season's change

dissolving
in an hour glass
one grain at a time

flakes become drops
absorbed
in unsatiated earth

thirsty
for the dissolution
of all lives

once lived.

Graveyard Fog

among the trees
wall shadows
still–nothing moving
in this world
unspun

stuck–in a rut become
tomb
skeletal ghosts
forgotten
but on nights like these

drink the blood
one drop at a time
savor the once lived
never alive

where did they go?
where do they go?
were they ever here?
ever?

suspended
hung
breathe it in
breathe it all in

taste the mercury bones
left behind

suck the marrow
there is no end

no voice
no song
no children laughing

not even the sun
for days
shedding pale fairytales

nobody
will ever hear

No Foxholes in Atheists

clouds form
on the horizon

an Armageddon army
advances

slow marching
consumes the sun

    sometimes things
    are not alright

    shadows drifting
    across the moon

    disfigured face
    becomes glare

a saltwater
dead man's float

submerged ears
drowning

sinking into the night
floating below

A Rain Thick Enough to Hue the Trees

what I observe from mostly under cover
baptized in memories lost, washing away
as the determined rivulets refuse retreat
and I realize night has befallen the sky
for the redwoods are no longer recognized
when a shiver whispers: what still can?

Bleed

Into my eyes, bring your demons to life
In me—Carve your name deep across my wrists
Make the pedophile sympathetic;
Give her the look like she might steal your babe,
But replace it with something you really
Wanted, instead. Tell me not quite a lie:
    All which remains is all that's gone too far.

Omen

All the wood is inside—Good thing, too. It
Rained last night, the wind howled. I will collect
The branches blown around the yard, add them
To the pile—after.

The sun isn't up, might not rise today
Clouds are slithering overhead—a snake
Pit in the sky. There's an opening in
The woods, a shadowed arch calling—I feel
I should 'vestigate.

September Morning

The wasp's shadow startled before it's plink
on the glass jarred me.

It's like the sun is using the window
as a magnifying glass over ants,
on me.

The white oak leaves pixilate against the
infant blue sky—dusted with contented
clouds, light and gentle in their lumbering.

I ate an apple off the ground today
Yesterday, it was from the tree.

I must confess: the one cradled in the
grass this morning far exceeded, in taste
and texture, the apple plucked from its branch.

That one was starchy.

The Grasshopper and the Post

A weathered post secures the clothes line, outside
My study window. An identical weathered post
Secures the clothes line above the yard at the edge of
The apple orchard. I have not seen the woodpecker
For a while, however, I have watched a grasshopper
Climb the weathered post closest the window, approach
The largest, quarter-sized hole, circle the shadow, then
Retreat to disappear among the blades of grass.

Leaving but a Shell

I don't understand Junebugs—well, a lot
Of things—but today it's Junebugs. The way
They buzz haphazardly, always into
Someone's hair, into the screen, the porch mat,
Then quit. The way they crunch under foot—is
It only the shell or do they have bones?
Their dark smear, sticky and orange and green-ish.
Not to mention their abandoned exo-
Skeletons: The legs and pinchers frozen
Jurassic in pose; back split from the eyes
Down; tiny white braids of tissues reaching
For whatever escaped to become—what?

Liturgy

on nights when I forget to feel afraid
the flame lights, before the stars
ignite the
canopy, and Saturn lures
while a lone
plane traverses the sky…

and then it's dark
and the woods crack under wandering hoof
and the mosquitos are forgotten, and
only remembered by the occasional itch
and I sip my wine, fill another glass
and the need to howl reaches its
repose,
so I do
elongated and
proud
and the wind stays the moment, and the
crickets chime in
and I hear the ohm reach
distant hills and return
as the trees growl
their response and, and…

it's nothing ever
recorded in symphony
the breaking
of earth's current over land
blowing on

my face
and ears
and provoking the hairs
on my neck to stand erect
and, nothing
to matter
less the realization that
nothing matters
poised by the flickering
flame, I light a cigarette…and the stars
disappear above the blanketing clouds
that weren't here a minute ago
which might
suggest rain
which we haven't had in days
which the sunflowers, now hung admit want
of, which the quitting grass underfoot scream
for, which…

I hadn't noticed the fire's
distillation
until it erupted
anew from the ashes
urging twice a
new howl—another homily

and I know, I am here
as the world sleeps
as I imagine the world sleeps
as a single mother beds her fatherless
children and worries about tomorrow's fare…
as Dorthy drifts away and before she clicks her heels
as I remember

what it is to remember
what is to remember
what doesn't
what isn't
what might have been bookended
between mass, then…

The Moon Is a River

always new
two fingers above the pines
east

I stand without flame
shade my eyes when
it ignites between clouds

ashamed
not enough to bow my head
and think: I should kneel

how many lives?
how many dreams?

how perspective changes
everything.

offer a prayer
—silent, as prayers
tend to be

selfish, determined
I am anew—again
bathed incandescently

I do not fear the forest
or the trees

offered in earnest
like each before
tomorrow begins at sunrise

She's Awake

The clamor of drawers opened, rummaged, closed
The creak of a worn bedspring under shifting
Pressure reverberates through the floor.

She's awake. That much I am certain—
And means she will be down here soon.

Not even in the room and already her *ff* cloud
Drowns the endowed *mezzo* rain, which
renews my soul beyond the pane.

Sunrise

The moment my life had prepared me for
And ill equipped—for how should it be that
I live while the entire world dies?

Finally

The birds have returned, the jays
Raping the feeder as they did in spring—
Before we blew it up on an acid

Infused eve. There were no birds this summer
Even with the new feeder erect in place
Where the old one stood.

Now it's fall, third day according to the calendar.
The leaves are turning amber, pumpkin and gold
The rains have arrived in welcome showers
The garden is harvested, the apples have fallen
And finally, the birds are back.

The jay's at least.
Attempting to rape the feeder as they had,
However, this new model: cylindrical,
¾ inch posts, tiny lip for a feeding tray—
Is too small for the aggressive jays—

But they are persistent, Green Eggs and Ham
Kind of birds: one wing gyrating
For balance; beak pecking desperately
At seed. Falling off, circling around, perching
Atop the post, determined to claim its bounty—

Personal Development

This time last year, I *could* have killed you.
Now I only *want* you dead—you and your
Parents; your aunts, uncles, your siblings;
fuck it, your dogs, too.
I think this is progress, Babe.

Le Monde

It demands much effort to suppress
The recognition of the vastness of
My ignorance and the depression it
Ushers—distractions, yes, they work
Best. See: What?

Admiration

Alabaster thread stitched thrice
A blank leather-bound journal—
An acme, completely unnerving
to cause even
The most resolved man to weep.
      —Would you?

The Moon Is a City Muting the Night

Outshining antiquated stars at peace.
Commanding as a moth to 'suming flame,
—If I stare long enough, will I, too, be
Muted?

Perfect Circles

I don't stare often enough at the moon.
even tonight, knowing this, I turned my gaze

why would I stare at the moon
when I can't stomach the face in the mirror?

cratered and sometimes bright, a face, mine
daily overcome by the creeping shadow

longing for the completing darkness
to dissolve what was into a gentle glowing ring

Right Now

I wish I were a god
if only to laugh at
all the reasons
we seek in earnest
to be bothered over

The Great Bachelor

For very long I set about being melancholy,
Convinced myself of sad thoughtfulness—
Alas, this is no use. I am well, here.
Sleep when am 'roused to sleep, eat
When the stomach desires, drink on tout
Of thirst, smoke in a chain if so compelled
—And all the others which accompany
This passage into new identity—Ecclesiastes.

Invitation

the moon pulses aflame
behind noctilucent clouds

ephemeral as a glimpse

while the gravity of voice
claws away at the day

settling in deathly horizon

The End is Always

Me,
by my
own
hands.